GOOD ∗ OLD ∗ DAYS®

Live It Again™
1940

The Saturday Evening Post

Volume 212, Number 44

April 27, 1940

5c. the Copy

U.S. CENSUS

Norman Rockwell

Dear Friends,

We were probably naïve. When 1940 dawned, many Americans entered the new decade with a sense of optimism, confidence and, yes, naïveté.

After all, we were more than 10 years removed from Black Tuesday and the Wall Street stock market crash of Oct. 29, 1929. While the economy wasn't back to the giddy days of the Roaring Twenties, industry and retail markets were definitely on the upswing. Gone were the dust storms of the Dirty Thirties. Franklin Delano Roosevelt was completing his second term as president (and would be reelected to an unprecedented third term in November).

As FDR's campaign song intoned: "Happy Days Are Here Again!"

But our days of renewed hope were shrouded with the reality of Hitler's hordes pushing at will across the European continent. The Blitz of Britain began in September and most of us somehow knew that the United States would sooner or later be drawn into the global conflagration.

As FDR's campaign song intoned: "Happy Days Are Here Again!"

Perhaps nothing illustrated the pivotal year of 1940 better than—of all things—women's hosiery. The modern miracle of the first nylon stockings went on sale in mid-May. Women excitedly replaced their fragile silk stockings with the wonderful new product. Less than a year later, commercial production of women's stockings was suspended as both silk and nylon were commandeered for the war effort. It would be 1947 before nylons were generally available again.

Perhaps the naïveté of early 1940 was doomed. But war was still nearly two years away. God-given rains and the resulting crops in the heartland were once again greening up Mother Earth. The great American industrial machine was whirling to life. As this collection of articles and photos so poignantly illustrates, the American spirit of optimism and confidence refused to succumb to the onslaught of time and circumstance. "Happy days"—albeit short-lived—were indeed here again!

Contents

© 1940 THE NORMAN ROCKWELL FAMILY ENTITIES

WIKIMEDIA PUBLIC DOMAIN PHOTOGRAPH

REPRINTED WITH PERMISSION FROM THE FORD MOTOR COMPANY

© 1940 SEPS

© 1940 SEPS

© 1940 SEPS

The local dime store was a popular spot for shopping and catching up with neighbors. Many had balconies, and children loved to scurry upstairs to watch other visitors from above.

Neighbors always found time to stop and chat over freshly made donuts and a cup of coffee.

Parks were cheap and enjoyable places for family picnics, rides on the park trains and sharing in family activities.

© 1940 SEPS

Everyday Life

Around town

Everyday life around town in 1940 was one of mixed emotions. The country was starting to slowly emerge from the hard work and concerns of the Great Depression. However, the mood was slightly subdued with the worry about what could be looming on the horizon with the rise of Adolph Hitler and the Third Reich.

It was a time of much enjoyment of neighbors, and friendly chats at the general store. Children and families found pleasure in going to the park for picnics and play. Friends and neighbors shared and bartered with each other for small needs and everyday supplies.

Drugstore soda fountains provided good gathering places after school and on warm summer afternoons. It was also a great place to treat a prospective girlfriend to an ice cream or a soda.

© 1940 SEPS

Children, filled with energy and a bit of orneriness, sometimes ended up helping with chores and small jobs.

© 1940 SEPS

Everyday Life
Winter activities

Skiing was a popular winter sport and often the reason for winter travel. Western ski resorts began to be a fashionable destination for vacationers.

"Sometimes I think it's more fun than skiing."

It didn't cost anything to have a "snow date," just some time and lots of help from Mother Nature. Frolicking in the snow often led to warm hearts.

A day on the ice often led to a game of crack the whip, which inevitably ended with someone sliding into a snow bank, like the young lad on the left.

THE SATURDAY EVENING POST

EMERY CLARKE

The Metro Daily News

FINAL EDITION

THE WEATHER

JANUARY 1940

OSKAR SCHINDLER BEGINS PROVIDING REFUGE FOR KRAKOW JEWS

Everyday Life

First crush to young love

Gifts that captured a woman's heart represented more simple times. A box of chocolates, an attractive necklace, flowers or a special gesture were all signals of attraction from one heart to the other.

The old saying, "The way to a man's heart is through his stomach," was often the case in response. Visits topped off by a homemade chocolate cake or a home-cooked meal invitation were always ways of saying, "I'm interested in you."

Moments together ranged from sitting on the front porch swing to attending an outdoor movie or taking a walk in the park.

REPRINTED WITH PERMISSION FROM RUSSELL STOVER CANDIES

© 1940 SEPS

KELLY TIRES REPRINTED WITH PERMISSION FROM THE GOODYEAR TIRE & RUBBER COMPANY

A colorful broach or necklace spoke many words and even made eyes a little dreamy for the special occasion.

Meeting barefooted by the family gate was always a good place for two young hearts to make first impressions.

A pretty corsage, from an admiring man, was a thoughtful gift for a young lady before a night on the town.

Studying together might have worked for the girl, but her attractiveness was often a bit distracting for a fellow experiencing his first crush.

A fashionable hat was an essential finishing touch to a stylish outfit.

"Something comfortable enough to shop for something fashionable in."

Easter

Everyday Life

1940s style

Dress in the early 1940s was often designed according to looks rather than comfort. Men wore wool suits while women wore uncomfortable dresses in order to fit in with the styles. Hats and styled hair were considered requirements, even for an everyday activity like going shopping or to work.

Heavy clothing was often worn in hot weather or in warm settings. Due to the cost of clothing, many of the garments, especially ladies', were homemade.

Manners were a very important part of social intermingling; ladies would curtsy and men would remove their hats in respect to the presence of women.

A woman properly attired with dress and hairstyle could often attract the attention of nearby men.

© 1940 SEPS

Everyday Life

On the town

A night on the town was an elegant affair. Men dressed in suits and ties—more formal occasions called for tuxedos—while women donned their best dresses and accessories. Tie racks full of ties were a common fixture in most men's closets, while most ladies had an array of choices in shoes and hats.

For the more formal events, bow ties and slicked down hair were a man's way of accompanying women in formal dresses with their best jewelry on display.

Social outings included everything from card parties to Friday nights at the skating rink or movies. Attending a dance facilitated by big band sounds was always a nice way to spend the evening for married couples, dates or those searching for friendship.

"Fixing up to go out" was the accepted standard in the early 1940s. In some cases, "competitive dressing" was a part of a subtle unspoken upsmanship for party wear.

Roller skating became a popular activity for dates, as well as school and church outings. Even there, men usually dressed in suits and ties while women dressed a bit more casual.

© 1940 SEPS

A mixture of formal dress, alcohol and good eating provided light spirits in the midst of a nation enjoying an increase in prosperity as it came out of the Great Depression.

Musical entertainment was expected at a nightclub. Often clubs paid generously for well-known singers and dancers, knowing that the investment would pay off with the customers that stars would attract.

Formal dancing, accompanied by the big band sounds of the day, was always a good way to conclude a celebrative event.

Tops at the Box Office

Boom Town

Fantasia

His Girl Friday

Kitty Foyle

Knute Rockne All American

My Favorite Wife

Northwest Passage

Pinocchio

Pride & Prejudice

Rebecca

Santa Fe Trail

Strange Cargo

The Grapes of Wrath

The Mark of Zorro

At the Movies

1940 brought big icons and unforgettable films from many different genres to the silver screen. Cary Grant displayed his star power in two popular romantic comedies, *The Philadelphia Story* and *His Girl Friday*. Adventure films took audiences on a journey to exotic lands and different times, far from their own realities.

However, not all of the films that year lured moviegoers to escape. John Ford's adaptation of *The Grapes of Wrath* beautifully portrayed the harsh realities of the Dust Bowl and Ginger Roger's portrayal of a hardworking girl in *Kitty Foyle* showed the dangers that faced a young girl on her own in New York.

Other adaptations of novels like the classic *Pride & Prejudice* and the dark mystery *Rebecca*, both starring Laurence Olivier, were also hits at the box office.

"I had two colossal dreams last night."

In *The Philadelphia Story*, Katherine Hepburn's character, Tracy Lord, gains insight during her humorous encounters with the varied characters in the film. Cary Grant plays Lord's ex-husband, and uses his wit to deliver memorable lines like "With the rich and mighty, always a little patience," to sum up the film's repeating theme of the need for understanding in relationships. Jimmy Stewart shines in his Academy award-winning role as writer/journalist who, despite his biting cynicism, appeals to the audience as a likeable character.

At the Movies

Ginger Rogers earned the Academy Award for Best Actress for her role as the title character in *Kitty Foyle*. One of Rogers' dresses in the film became so iconic that after the release of the film, the dress style was referred to as "Kitty Foyle."

Alfred Hitchcock's cinematic take on Daphne Du Maurier's novel *Rebecca* won two Academy Awards, including Best Picture. The leading man, Laurence Olivier, did not treat his leading lady, Joan Fontaine, well because he wanted his then-girlfriend, Vivian Leigh, to play her part. Director Hitchcock took advantage of the situation by telling Fontaine that everyone on the set disliked her, which affected her acting by making her character more nervous, exactly what Hitchcock wanted for the role.

The Grapes of Wrath, John Ford's adaptation of John Steinbeck's Pulitzer Prize-winning novel, illustrated the plight of thousands of "Okies" forced, by the horrible conditions of the Dust Bowl, to leave their land in Oklahoma in search of a new life. The film inspired Woody Guthrie's two-part song "Tom Joad" (1940) as well as Bruce Springsteen's "The Ghost of Tom Joad" (1995).

©GETTY IMAGES

In the comedy *His Girl Friday*, Rosalind Russell's Hildy proves to be a match to Cary Grant's Walter, a fellow reporter. The film is notorious for the rapid-fire and witty banter that flies between Hildy and Walter.

WIKIMEDIA PUBLIC DOMAIN PHOTOGRAPH

Animation

Animation, a previously uncommon medium in film, became much more prevalent in 1940. Most of this notoriety was due to the release of two animated feature-length films from the Walt Disney Company. *Pinocchio*, released in February of that year, introduced the enduring Disney character Jiminy Cricket who sang the song "When You Wish Upon a Star." The song became such a hit that it was more popular than the film. Disney also released the film *Fantasia*, which was first shown as a "roadshow" film, opening only in select cities and select theaters with reserved seating before several re-releases in the following years.

Disney was not the only company to produce animated films that year. William Hanna and Joseph Barbera introduced the characters Tom and Jerry in the animated short *Puss Gets the Boot*. Warner Brothers' *Looney Tunes* was also popular with moviegoers.

One of the most notable aspects of the film *Fantasia* is the classical music score. Outside of some short introductions for each piece, there is no dialogue in the film. All eight musical pieces were recorded under the direction of composer Leopold Stowkowski, shown above with Walt Disney. Seven of eight of the pieces were performed by the Philadelphia Orchestra, shown with Stowkowski below.

Hanna and Barbera formed a lasting partnership and wrote and directed over 160 short animated films during the years 1940–1967 using the characters Tom and Jerry.

©GETTY IMAGES

Fantasia was initially a financial disappointment for Disney. Many moviegoers did not respond well to the first release of the long, animated film, even with its appeal of being the first major film to feature stereophonic sound. However, in subsequent years the film was edited several times, and eventually became one of the most noted and classic of all of Disney's films.

What Made Us Laugh

"The page on 'swallowing things' must be one of the ones he ate!"

"I can't do a thing with him. Our governess is on vacation and I don't speak a word of French."

"He came over and asked if he could be of any assistance."

"Stand still, Junior, or the nice man will think you want him to give mother his seat."

"But I don't want him to come back a man! I want him to come back mother's same darling little boy!"

"But, Sonny—your Uncle Harry only complained of a slight cold."

"We're sort of worried about him, doctor. Last night he said he wanted to grow up to be Vice-President."

"I am counting to a hundred, but I want him around when I finish."

The Goodness of Grandparents

The integral role of grandparents in family dynamics was immeasurable in a time when they often lived within the family unit or were as close as the place down the road.

Grandchildren often learned how to cook by working in the kitchen with their grandmothers. Life's lessons were often imparted through wisdom received from gardening or working with Grandpa on various family projects.

While teaching grandchildren how to knit, sew or do wood projects, grandparents also told stories from the family heritage. Grandchildren loved to gather around their grandparents to hear tales of how things were in days gone by. Grandparents' wisdom and stories were treasured by their grandchildren, who would remember the family lore for future years.

© 1940 THE NORMAN ROCKWELL FAMILY ENTITIES

Time spent with grandparents fostered the spirit of family dynamics that would reach toward the next generation when grandchildren passed them on to their own families.

REPRINTED WITH PERMISSION FROM THE GOODYEAR TIRE & RUBBER COMPANY

REPRINTED WITH PERMISSION FROM GENERAL MOTORS

The love between parents and grandparents provided an example to young grandchildren of how to treat others.

Nothing beat the perfection of Grandma's cakes and way of cooking. The expression "this tastes just like Grandma's," immediately resurrects memories of taste and aroma from a bygone era.

FAMOUS BIRTHDAYS
Fran Tarkenton, February 3 Football Player
Tom Brokaw, February 6 News Anchor
Ted Koppel, February 8 News Anchor

The Goodness of Grandparents

Grandmas had a special way of doctoring sore throats and childhood illnesses with remedies from bygone days. Just the fact that it came from Grandma seemed to give recovery a head start.

Grandpa's observations sank deep in the soul of young grandsons who felt that their grandparents knew everything about life.

FAMOUS BIRTHDAYS
Smokey Robinson, February 19
Musician
Peter Fonda, February 23 Actor

Grandma always seemed to have a needle and thread handy to fix britches, darn socks and sew buttons back on shirts or coats.

Children often
believed
that their
grandmother
could do
anything,
including
blowing up a
football that
needed a little
extra air.

Everyday Life

From the market to the table

During the Great Depression, many families were very independent in bringing in the family meals through gardening, bartering vegetables, and stretching flour and sugar products around the family meal table.

With the Depression over, 1940 consumer food intake became more dependent on the increasing market for canned foods such as soup, meat and vegetables. With the increase in cross-country transportation, and the rising availability of fuel, fresh fruits and vegetables from all parts of the nation were more available at the local market.

Community supermarkets began to replace the old general store, often enticing customers with giveaways such as free plates, utensils and other household items.

"H'm'm'm, smells good! What was it?"

The idea of men cooking was still foreign at the time, unless the cooking involved a grill and meat, when the man of the house took charge.

© 1940 SEPS

The addition of canned soups and other prepared retail foods added extra time for leisure or to do other chores.

Everyday Life
Sugar and spice and everything nice

Trying to eat an apple without getting juice on a nice dress wasn't always the easiest thing for a girl looking at the world through eyes of mischief.

FAMOUS BIRTHDAYS
Nancy Pelosi, March 26 Speaker of the House
Chuck Norris, March 10 Actor

Sowing seeds of mischief was always a temptation after sitting around for a certain length of time. The subtle smiles of these children reveal wandering thoughts of distraction.

The look in a daughter's eyes can go a long way in grabbing sympathy from a father's heart. Both father and daughter would enjoy their special moments together.

Imitating the local beautician with the family pet could cause a bigger mess than most mothers wanted to deal with.

Creative minds had no problem thinking of energy-filled activities when they assembled together.

Everyday Life

Snips and snails and puppy dog tails

Creativity was a big part of every child's life, especially with the lack of technology and innovation that would create forms of entertainment so prevalent in today's world.

Hitching a train ride, inventing neighborhood clubs and snatching hot baked goods were all ways of life for young creative minds.

Youthful energy often revealed itself in climbing trees, viewing the world from the house roof and taking on unsolicited "projects" around the property.

In the midst of it all, the boys held guiltless expressions such as was portrayed in the *Our Gang* comedy movies. For wise parents, that look was always an indication that "something was cooking" somewhere.

The neighborhood gang always had something creative up its sleeve, and the ornerier, the more the look of innocence. Many of these "projects" were planned in the midst of secret club meetings.

"Junior, have you been naughty again?"

"I'd like a breakfast cereal that would cut down his energy."

FAMOUS BIRTHDAYS
Herbie Hancock, April 12
Musician
Al Pacino, April 25 Actor

Everyday Life

Playtime in the neighborhood

Meeting a close friend for a roller skating expedition was always a good way to catch up on the latest gossip, or end up at the corner market for some penny candy.

Sports gear and other items facilitating childhood playtime activities were usually just inside the front door and ready for action.

In many neighborhoods, both boys and girls gathered for sandlot baseball, softball and basketball games. Roller skates and the latest model of bicycles were primary means of transportation to and from activities.

Sandboxes, pup tents and swing sets were common items designed to keep children in the neighborhood and in their own yards.

In the end, "creating activity" was often the most popular attraction; with that there was no end to the potential for fun.

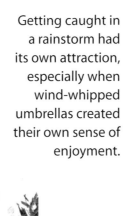

Getting caught in a rainstorm had its own attraction, especially when wind-whipped umbrellas created their own sense of enjoyment.

Exploration was another favorite pastime that often lead to fascinating discoveries not far from home.

When two boys were standing still contemplating, it would just be a matter of minutes before creative energy led to mischief.

A neighborhood game of baseball had to be put on hold when a young boy had to complete his chore of beating the dust out of a household rug.

Showing off a fancy new bike always brought its own sense of neighborhood status; it became the envy of every non-owner on the block.

The Metro Daily News

FINAL EDITION

APRIL 23, 1940

FIRE AT THE RHYTHM NIGHT CLUB

It leaves dozens dead in Natchez, Mississippi.

A calming and beautiful photograph of a plane above the clouds attracted potential air travellers.

Air Travel

Dreams of flight

Everyone was looking up in the early 1940s as the presence of air travel increased. The sound of an airplane would bring people out of their homes to watch the plane pass over in the sky. As the plane flew over residential areas, flight direction caused speculation over where the plane was coming from and where it was going.

One of the most heralded attractions of 1940 was an air show, which occurred increasingly often. Large crowds would gather at air fields to watch locals and professionals demonstrate their skills.

Many audience members were tempted to learn to fly their own small planes. Some of the smallest planes retailed for about the same price as a new car in 1940.

Even the cowboys of the largely unsettled West were not immune to feeling the shadow of a passing plane overhead.

Military equipment was being tested constantly to upgrade its performance.

The development of model airplanes opened up a whole new field of entertainment as model fliers sought to imitate what they were seeing in the sky.

The thought of flying over the mountaintops and higher than the clouds was a storybook reality for some of the first souls to enjoy air travel in the early 1940s.

Air Travel

Takes off

As flights became more available, business people began to take advantage of the convenience and speed of air travel.

Although longer flights were still quite expensive, shorter flights between cities were a little more affordable. These shorter flights encouraged more people to choose air travel for business, which would cut down their transit times significantly.

Even the sporting world began to look to the skies for its travel. On November 17, the Green Bay Packers became the first team to travel by air.

1940 and now

TWA FIRST TO BRING YOU:
4 Engines!
Supercharged Cabin!
Overweather Flying!

Boeing

The TRANSCONTINENTAL Airline

TWA Stratoliner

TWA *Stratoliner*

High altitude **Outside**
Low altitude **Inside**
FLY OUT OF REACH OF EARTH-BOUND WEATHER!

TWA The TRANSCONTINENTAL Airline

© 1940 SEPS

"Please be calm—there's absolutely no danger!"

AIR LINES

© 1940 SEPS

"And this is the gadget which, when it works, tells you whether all the other gadgets are working or not."

The idea of flying across the continent in style was a dream for many, but considered to be only for the rich and famous in its earliest stages.

Everyday Life

Staying connected

The thought of talking to someone at a distance and having an instant reply was still a fairly exciting idea to most people in 1940.

The ringing of the phone often brought a mad scramble from everyone in the house in an attempt to answer it first. In many neighborhoods, those who had purchased a phone first became the "headquarters" of phone calls for neighbors who hadn't made the investment yet.

Party, or shared, lines kept everyone in the loop, as those on the line could quietly listen to any conversation at hand. In the case of switchboard operators, information could be passed to many homes at one time by the prompting of the switchboard plugs.

Initially, the phone numbers of those on a party line were differentiated by the number of rings a call prompted. Everyone on the line memorized everyone else's ring, thus knowing who calls were being made to immediately.

The opportunity to talk to loved ones at a distance, especially on holidays and birthdays, provided a sense of comfort to curious relatives who constantly wondered how their loved ones were doing.

Business people began to use the phone to set up and confirm appointments.

FAMOUS BIRTHDAYS
Ricky Nelson, May 8 Musician
and Actor
Toni Tennille, May 8 Singer

A father who was about to leave on a business trip could comfort his son by reminding the boy that his father was only a call away.

© 1940 SEPS

September 7, 1940 was considered to be the first German Blitz in London. It was followed by a week of almost uninterrupted air-raid attacks in different parts of London that left the city devastated. Hundreds of buildings were destroyed and the first significant civilian casualties of the war were counted.

NARA, ARC 541917

On May 14, 1940 the first appeal for enlistment in the Local Defense Volunteers went out over the radio waves, calling for older men who were not active in Britain's military forces. The LDV eventually became the Home Guard, a strong group of civilian men who prepared to defend England's borders against a possible German invasion. The Home Guard was also important during air raids on British cities. Shown at right, an aircraft spotter performs his duty on a rooftop overlooking London and St. Paul's Cathedral.

NARA, ARC 541899

War in Europe

England at war

1940 was a pivotal year for England in World War II. For the first half of the year, British soldiers were mostly stationed in other countries or at sea to help prevent the Germans from taking control of Europe. But on July 10, the war hit home when Germany began bombing Britain's factories and military facilities. Then in September, Hitler lifted his ban on bombing British cities and the air raid Blitzes began and continued off and on throughout the year, destroying many parts of cities. Even Buckingham Palace was not spared from the damage of a German bomb. Many British people chose to stay in their city homes; however, many children were sent away to reside with other families living in rural England.

LIBRARY OF CONGRESS, PRINTS AND PHOTOGRAPHS DIVISION

British Prime Minister Winston Churchill visits the devastated St. Michael's Cathedral, later rebuilt as Coventry Cathedral, following the November 14–15 Blitz on Coventry.

UNITED KINGDOM GOVERNMENT, IMPERIAL WAR MUSEUM COLLECTIONS

The Metro Daily News

THE WEATHER
City and Suburbs,
Snow, Colder

FINAL EDITION

VOLUME 41—No. 161

FIVE CENTS

20 PAGES

MAY 10, 1940

WINSTON CHURCHILL BECOMES PRIME MINISTER OF BRITAIN

Between May 27 and June 4, over 300,000 French and British soldiers were evacuated from Dunkirk in a flotilla of every conceivable type of boat, including privately-owned small pleasure craft to commercial fishing boats and ferries that would shuttle troops to the larger military ships waiting offshore.

War in Europe
Occupied nations

As Hitler and his forces marched west, more and more European countries fell to Axis control. On March 12, Europe lost Finland when it conceded territory to the USSR in a peace treaty. A month later, on April 9, Denmark was forced to surrender to Germany. On May 10, Hitler began a large scale invasion of Europe that included Belgium, France, Luxembourg and the Netherlands. Five days later, the Netherlands surrendered to Germany. Soon after, on May 28, Belgium fell to German control, followed by Norway on June 10. German troops then headed to France and established power.

During these months, British troops gave their support to their Northern European neighbors, but were forced to retreat at the end of May from Dunkirk.

© 1940 SEPS

After the May invasion, German troops began to gain more control of France and entered Paris on June 14. By June 22, France formally surrendered to Germany. In July, after the surrender, a French Nazi government known as Vichy France was established. German soldiers, like those shown above, enjoyed free reign in Paris.

Although 1940 involved many European surrenders to Axis powers, there were other nations, like Greece, that were able to fight occupation. On October 28, Italian forces invaded Greece, but the Greek army held its ground and by November 14, the invasion had been repelled. Greek soldiers, like the one shown here, were grateful to elude Axis control.

The Metro Daily News

THE WEATHER
City and State—Rain
Snow, Colder

FINAL
EDITION

VOLUME 97 — No. 181

FIVE CENTS

MAY 15, 1940

THE FIRST NYLON STOCKINGS GO ON SALE.

Czechoslovakia, among the few presenters who were under Axis control in 1940, ran its exhibit with particular nationalistic pride, as did other occupied nations like Poland and France. The mural above decorated the Czech exhibit.

The World's Fair featured many sculptures, among them this intricate carving by Malvina Hoffman titled "Dances of the Races."

Some exhibits, like the Italian Pavilion, fused the old with the new. Here, elements of ancient Rome are juxtaposed with modern elements, like the 200-foot high waterfall that covered a full wall of the Italian façade.

The fair was organized with several differently themed "zones" that flowed out from a central area, as the above photograph shows.

World's Fair

The 1939–1940 World's Fair was held at Flushing Meadows-Corona Park in New York and was the largest world's fair of all time. It was a giant undertaking that took four years of preparation for the planning, organizing and building of all its exhibits. With the slogan "Dawn of a New Day," the fair offered visitors a glimpse of the "world of tomorrow." It featured exhibits like Voder, a keyboard-operated speech synthesizer, color photography, nylon, air conditioning, the View-Master and the later unsuccessful Smell-O-Vision, among many others.

This World's Fair housed exhibits from many nations and was the largest international event since World War 1, a fact that drastically changed the focus of the fair in its second season. With the advent of the conflict in Europe, some participants did not return in 1940 and the theme of the fair was changed to "For Peace and Freedom."

The Chrysler, Ford and General Motors companies all created exhibits in the "Transportation Zone" that displayed experimental product ideas that most likely would become available in the following years. The international focus of the World's Fair was evidenced even among commercial exhibits, as can be seen in the photograph of the Chrysler Motors Building above.

Holland, another country that fell prey to Axis occupation in 1940, displayed a garden proudly bursting with its iconic flower, the tulip.

World's Fair

Facts & Figures

- It covered 1,216 acres.

- Over its two seasons, it received over 45 million visitors.

- It created the Westinghouse Time Capsule, which was not to be opened until 5,000 years after its burial in 1939. The capsule contained items as diverse as writings from Einstein to a kewpie doll and a pack of cigarettes.

- On July 4, 1940, the Fair hosted "Superman Day" and hired Ray Middleton to act the part, the first time anyone had played the role of Superman.

- The designer of the USSR Pavilion, Alexey Dushkin, won the Grand Prize for the Fair with his life-size copy of the interior of the Mayakovskaya station of the Moscow Metro.

- The official colors of the fair were blue and orange, the colors of New York City.

- The fair was pivotal in promoting the production of the first fluorescent lights.

- The fair opened on April 30, 1939 and officially closed on October 27, 1940.

- The fair generated about $48 million dollars; however, the Fair Corporation had invested $67 million dollars into the project, so it was considered a financial failure.

- Germany was the only major power of the time that did not participate.

The fair's Government Zone housed both the "Halls of Nations" and the "Court of States," seen here across a reflecting pool.

Part of the "Hall of Nations" was the British Pavilion, which displayed a copy of the Magna Carta. This copy, belonging to Lincoln Cathedral, had never left Britain before. When the fair ended, it was decided it was safer to keep the copy in the United States to avoid damage during air raids in Britain during World War II. The copy remained at Fort Knox until 1947.

Several aspects of the fair were not strictly educational. Heineken's on the Zuider Zee contained four restaurants, a bar and provided musical entertainment for guests.

The "Theme Center" of the World's Fair held two striking, all-white buildings. The Trylon stood over 700 feet tall. The Perisphere was a large sphere that could be accessed by a curved walkway called the Helicline. In the Perisphere, visitors could view a model "city of tomorrow" while standing on an elevated moving walkway. The buildings provided an impressive center to the fair.

The Consolidated Edison Building "City of Light" offered not only a dramatic water fountain to entertain visitors, but also a show using music, sound effects and synchronized narration to illustrate Consolidated Edison's work with steam, gas and electricity.

What Made Us Laugh

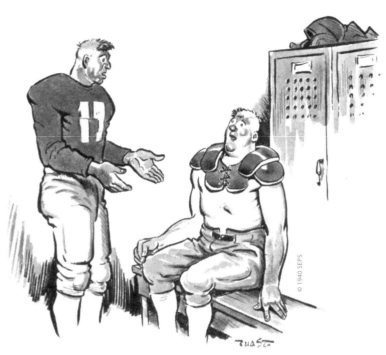

"Nowadays you practically need a college education to play tackle."

"An' smart as a whip too! Come here all the way from 'Frisco—alone!"

"I don't see any soaring poetry of motion."

"No—we found my ball. We've lost the golf course."

"Oh, some petty quarrel, I imagine."

"Aw, gee! Coach! You wouldn't want me
for a center. Shucks! I'm no good."

"Don't let her fool you. That's just a come-on. I
lost ten bucks on her that way last week."

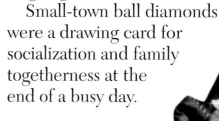
© 1940 SEPS

Batter Up

Everyone plays

The popularity of baseball rapidly spread from the traditional major leagues to other cultures and countries. While baseball developed overseas in countries like Japan, the Negro National League at home became extremely popular. Such teams as the Washington Homestead Grays (league champions), Baltimore Elite Giants and Newark Eagles became major drawing cards wherever they played.

The popularity of baseball leagues for children continued to grow. Young aspiring baseball players from small towns imagined that they were filling the shoes of their favorite major league greats.

Small-town ball diamonds were a drawing card for socialization and family togetherness at the end of a busy day.

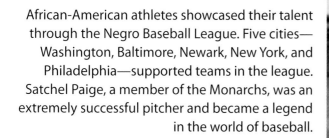

African-American athletes showcased their talent through the Negro Baseball League. Five cities—Washington, Baltimore, Newark, New York, and Philadelphia—supported teams in the league. Satchel Paige, a member of the Monarchs, was an extremely successful pitcher and became a legend in the world of baseball.

©GETTY IMAGES/MAJOR LEAGUE BASEBALL

THE SATURDAY EVENING POST

From sandlots to major league ball parks, everyone enjoyed America's favorite game, baseball.

© 1940 SEPS

© 1940 SEPS

THE SATURDAY
EVENING ST

On the Gridiron

College football reigned supreme in 1940. The early popularity of college coaches such as Knute Rockne, plus the attention drawn by the bowl games, captured every sports fan's attention to the college scene. The origin of certain offensive and defensive schemes by college coaches infiltrated the game on a nationwide basis.

The 1940 college football season ended with the University of Minnesota Golden Gophers being named the national champion and Stanford in second place. The Heisman Trophy winner was Michigan halfback Tom Harmon.

Bowl winners included: Sugar Bowl, Boston College; Orange Bowl, Mississippi State; Rose Bowl, USC, and Cotton Bowl, Texas A&M.

In the National Football League, the Chicago Bears (Western Division) defeated the Washington Redskins (Eastern Division) 73–0, in one of the most one-sided games in professional football history.

The biographical film of successful Notre Dame coach Knute Rockne, starring Ronald Reagan, was one of the most popular movies of the year.

"I always break the football enthusiasts in that way. Gradually they get used to the feel of books."

"Gee, Coach, I never dreamed you'd actually want me to play."

"You know, Jack, someday I'm going to get a nice little place inland, and a small car, and just ride to my heart's content!"

"My dear, if you've never been becalmed with a Yale man, you've never been becalmed at all."

The Metro Daily News
FINAL EDITION

JUNE 4, 1940

CHURCHILL DECLARES "WE SHALL NEVER SURRENDER"
He concludes during a speech to the House of Commons.

Fun on the Water

The rise of the economy from the Great Depression, enticed many Americans to find family and personal relaxation on popular lakes and various bodies of water.

From the Great Lakes to the Eastern inlets, sailboats, fishing boats, yachts and motorboats could be seen overspreading the waters, especially on weekends and holidays.

Many smaller inland lakes, in such places as Michigan, Indiana and Minnesota, were surrounded by cottages where those employed in metropolitan areas escaped for the weekend.

In the northern climates, water fun would convert into skiing and ice fishing, which would be equally popular during the winter months.

© 1940 SEPS

Boarding the yacht for major fishing expeditions took the effort of the family crew. Everyone joined in, including those who trolled the waters with rods and reels.

© 1940 SEPS

Whole days of relaxation were spent in various types of boats where those aboard would cook meals, fish or swim while the boat was anchored in the lakes.

© 1940 SEPS

Everyday Life

Traveling nation

As travel increased and vehicle ownership expanded, local service stations began to pamper their customers as a means of competing with other stations.

Service station owners would not only pump gasoline, they would also check vehicle fluids, clean the windshield and often clean all windows and mirrors.

Some station owners developed such a friendly relationship with clientele that they would give candy to children. Sometimes they would hand out small giveaways such as household items or tools.

"All right! Turn 'er off! She's still not right!"

Gasoline stations were full-service, with attendants putting in the gasoline, checking fluids and cleaning windows, all with a friendly smile during a quick visit.

Something a
lady appreciates...

New service-station facilities included inside
restrooms, still a novelty for many customers,
especially those from the rural areas.

Large service-station signs with flood lights
began to dot the countryside as a beckoning call,
advertising the local brand of gasoline.

Buick Super Model 51 Four-Door Touring Sedan

Yes Indeed !

"LONGEST of the LOT!"

and also the liveliest of all lowest-priced cars !

The Special De Luxe Sport Sedan, 2024

Chevrolet Special De Luxe Sport Sedan

Ford V-8

Cars

1940 was one of the most prolific years of automobile production in the decade, with carmakers turning out a total of 4,680,000 cars. Two years later, car production was shut down and stayed that way during the war years.

In the early 1940s, cars began to take on a lower, longer and broader look. This new look fit in well with the luxury cars that were beginning to be produced. These cars had high-end details that were meant to give the idea of status and wealth.

Pontiac
AMERICA'S FINEST LOW-PRICED CAR

1940 was the first and only year for the production of the Mercury 8.

"My First Olds took me to my first World's Fair!"

Many advertisers capitalized on the popularity and allure of the World's Fair in 1940, suggesting that attendance was easy as long as people had reliable cars to take them there.

"It was the greatest thrill of my life — that moment in 1904 when we started for the Louisiana Purchase Exposition in our Oldsmobile Curved Dash Runabout! It was only 170 miles from our town to St. Louis, but that was a major journey in those times. Needless to say, we made the round trip easily because our dependable Oldsmobile certainly lived up to its early-day slogan, *'Built to Run, and Does It!'*"

FROM AN UNRETOUCHED KODACHROME PHOTOGRAPH TAKEN AT THE "WORLD OF TOMORROW," NEW YORK

KODACHROME TAKEN AT "GOLDEN GATE INTERNATIONAL EXPOSITION," SAN FRANCISCO

"THIS YEAR, I'M SEEING TWO FAIRS *In My Merry Oldsmobile*"

TODAY, owners of Oldsmobile cars think nothing of motor trips that take them across the continent and back. Oldsmobile *performance* is so smooth and responsive that miles flow by like magic. Oldsmobile *handling* and Oldsmobile *riding* are so matchlessly easy and comfortable that even the longest day's run brings no fatigue. While Oldsmobile *dependability*, born in the late 1890's and solidly established over the years, gives never a cause for question! . . . To the 20,000 Olds owners whose 1940 cars are built with Oldsmobile's exclusive Hydra-Matic Drive, long journeys are a *double* delight. With *no gears to shift* and *no clutch to press*, driving is simplified by half. And with a special pick-up gear for passing and a special cruising speed for open road driving, performance is stepped up to an exciting new tempo! . . . If you, too, would like a thrilling and care-free trip to the Fairs, your Oldsmobile dealer can help you!

Visit General Motors' Exhibits at both New York and San Francisco

OLDSMOBILE *AMERICA'S OLDEST MOTOR CAR MANUFACTURER*

REPRINTED WITH PERMISSION FROM GENERAL MOTORS COMPANY

Cars

Cars began to take on a variety of shapes and sizes and were available in a rainbow of colors, all designed to catch the attention of the new car buyer.

In 1940, LaSalle introduced two model groups, the Series 50 conventional line and the more popular Series 52 line. The convertible coupe was one of the most highly regarded of the Series 52 line.

La Salle V8

Studebakers, like this 1940 Champion, were known for their wide variety of colors.

Lincoln Zephyr V-12

Packard Custom Super-8 180

REPRINTED WITH PERMISSION FROM STUDEBAKER NATIONAL MUSEUM

REPRINTED WITH PERMISSION FROM GENERAL MOTORS COMPANY

REPRINTED WITH PERMISSION FROM THE FORD MOTOR COMPANY

REPRINTED WITH PERMISSION FROM GENERAL MOTORS COMPANY

While mothers read stories on the beach, their children used creativity to build sand castles nearby.

Everyday Life

Summer fun

Much of the summer fun in 1940 centered around the family pond or fishing hole. Public swimming pools at the time were rare, but country ponds and public swimming areas at lakes allowed for plenty of splashes and a little mischief.

Tire inner tubes were utilized for everything from keeping non-swimmers afloat, to sunning relaxation and tugging behind boats.

Of course, swimwear was quite modest, and adults often sat around and soaked in the latest news while their children did cannonballs off the old wooden pier.

Other activities included making sand castles, finding creatures and critters, and enjoying a cool summer treat.

"All the neighbors back home sent us cards saying: 'Having a wonderful time, stay as long as you can.'"

Straw hats protected a person from the hot sun when adults sat around in sportswear and one-piece swimwear while they enjoyed a summer day.

Sunning in tilt-back lawn chairs required the most modest attire, including sport tops, casual slacks, socks and shoes. It was a good time to read and catch up on some of the latest magazines while dreaming of cooler weather.

Everyday Life

Outdoor style

Even for the most casual outdoor activities, modest dress was still the name of the game.

Time spent in the hot summer sun involved gleaning through magazines in sporty tops and pants or enjoying a picnic in a cotton dress. Even camping expeditions and retreats required white shirts, ties and the finest ladies' attire.

Even less formal occasions, like sporting activities, called for a well put-together outfit.

Sportswear was considerably more dressy in 1940. Ladies often wore skirts even while spending a day being active.

Sitting on the hillside in a favorite park and muching on homemade picnic food was always a good way to get better acquainted and allowed diners to dress somewhat more informally than they would at home or at a restaurant.

Young boys looked forward to spending time away from home at camp with their fellow Boy Scouts.

Everyday Life

Summer activities

The warmth of family closeness came together through picnics, Sunday afternoon drives and visits to such places of interest as the zoo and the local park. Others would spend their time playing outdoor sports, like tennis, to enjoy a summer day. Packing a lunch basket and heading out to the closest playground was always the highlight of the week.

Another seasonal tradition was going to summer camp. While many kids looked forward to meeting new friends and learning new skills, others missed their families, friends and that special someone back home. Summer camps offered a chance for kids to explore the outdoors and get the feeling of "roughing it" in the wilderness.

Outside games, such as tennis and other sports, played a prominent part in family life, wearing Dad out while the children improved their skills.

Coming home from camp often involved a unique combination of formal apparel, shin pads, packs of clothing, a plant, and of course, the new friendly turtle acquired along the way.

THE SATURDAY EVENING POST
An Illustrated Weekly
Founded A.D. 1728 by Benj. Franklin
August 24, 1940   5c. the Copy

Norman Rockwell

"Now, as soon as they land and start enjoying it, everybody come out and start pestering them."

One of the important moments of camp life was when mail arrived from home, especially from boyfriends or girlfriends at a distance.

CAMP WIP-PUR-WIL

U.S. MAIL

The Metro Daily News

FINAL EDITION

JUNE 22, 1940

DAIRY QUEEN OPENS FIRST STORE

There was plenty of hardware to pass out for the investment at some of the year's most expensive races.

FAMOUS BIRTHDAYS

Ringo Starr, July 7 Musician, The Beatles
Joe Torre, July 18 Baseball player & manager
Alex Trebek, July 22 Host of Jeopardy

Sport of Kings

Horseback riding

Horseback racing was tagged "the sport of kings" due to the amount of money involved and the cost of keeping and training a racehorse. Many races were social events where stylish men and ladies could "see and be seen." However, there were also many racing fans that weren't socialites and, instead, enjoyed the thrill of a close race.

Among those well-known horses of the time, Bimelech captured both the Preakness and Belmont Stakes in Triple Crown action, and Gallahadion was the winner of the Kentucky Derby.

In 1940, in his final race, Seabiscuit won $121,000 at the Santa Anita Handicap.

Horseback riding increased as a popular sport in local and state competition. Many young people spent much of their summer caring for and training their horses.

© 1940 SEPS

Racing legend Seabiscuit cuts the track in another money-making effort. The horse retired at a relatively young age after bringing in a winning total of $437,730 in 35 races.

The Metro Daily News

FINAL EDITION

JULY 8, 1940

FIRST COMMERCIAL FLIGHT USING PRESSURIZED CABINS
The plane flies from New York to Burbank, California.

© 1940 SEPS

"The back straight, Mrs. Quinn; heels down and slightly in; the arms loose at the sides, grasping the reins lightly between the thumb and first finger."

What Made Us Laugh

"Come now…surely <u>one</u> of you can think of a
reason why this wedding should not go on!"

"I got him through a matrimonial agency.
They were having a clearance."

"We want to renew our license
for another year."

"She finally decided she would marry Mr. Shilling.
I lost out in the semifinals."

The weaker sex.

"Well, here's my dollar!"

Everyday Life

Love and marriage

Weddings in the 1940s were often private, less elaborate and held with little fanfare. It was not unusual to be married in a minister's living room, or with a small party in the front of the church.

Weddings involving those in military service were often held during brief furloughs, sometimes in the family home or backyard.

Although the country was beginning to prosper more, most Americans didn't have the funds or time to put into large weddings with much pomp and preparation.

Honeymoons were often much more simple, perhaps a one- or two-day trip to a lake cottage or resort. Very few couples traveled on long trips or out of the country.

Not every wedding involved wedding gowns or formal attire. Many couples were married in traditional dress-up clothes.

"I love you, Eve." "I love you, too, Sidney."

The more wealthy of the time would have much more elaborate ceremonies, complete with the most expensive gowns.

For those in military service, the time between deciding to marry and carrying out the ritual was often quite short.

When formal weddings occurred, decorations were lavish and the bride and groom were in the utmost formal attire. Even then, wedding parties were quite often limited to family and best friends.

Young couples often enjoyed a quiet evening together taking a walk or sitting on the front porch.

"But it's only for a short while, darling. Until we can get two seats together."

"With our unit,
all you have to
buy is three walls
and a roof."

Everyday Life

Making a house a home

During the break between the Great Depression and World War II, the birth of modern conveniences began; they quickly made their way into American households.

Appliances such as electric stoves, freezers and more modern refrigerators began to reach a price range where they were more affordable to those of modest income.

Homeowners made other changes to make their homes more modern. Kitchen cabinets were connected to provide more counter top space for new appliances. In addition, living rooms needed to accommodate the record players and radios, which were large in size.

Many sweepers were sold by door-to-door salesmen. Names such as Electrolux and Kirby became household brands.

PREMIER VAC-KIT

FOR DIRT ZONE
No. 2
—the deep pile of
all rugs and carpets—
the PREMIER
FLOOR CLEANER!

PREMIER

Many husbands turned a worried eye on their wives when they considered changing their homes' decor. Fabric swatches and paint chips could mean a considerable expense in the future.

"Could you come over this afternoon and bring your tools?"

Plain color variations of gray or darker suits and dresses, which were often decorated with lace, were considered stylish clothing. A pipe often added a bit of sophistication to a man's image.

A good bottle of wine or cup of tea enjoyed close to a fireplace often brought about a relaxed setting for family discussion.

Everyday Life

At home in style

Entertaining guests at the time often involved dressing formally and stylishly for an elaborate dinner followed by drinks or coffee in front of the fireplace. Wine often enhanced the atmosphere of a dinner party, as did candlelight and softly played big band music. A family dinner was more casual, but suits and dresses were still expected for the evening meal.

Smoking pipes was in style; discussion with the smell of pipe smoke was often considered well-seasoned, especially when it took place with those dressed in the stylish clothing of the day.

Couples in formal attire listened to favorite programs on the radio as the gentle aroma of fresh cut flowers softened the atmosphere.

"It's rumored that she's after her grandfather's money."

Everyday Life
Family time

Family life in the country involved a blended time of work, play and creative fun. There was plenty of "home time" to enjoy each other and learn how to get along with others.

REPRINTED WITH PERMISSION OF AGFA ANSCO

"Have you <u>anything</u> that doesn't <u>always</u> end up in a fight?"

"We're saving the expense of going to a summer resort this season!"

Camping was one of the primary ways of getting away as a family to have fun. Quite often, this was as simple as packing food in a basket and taking a tent to a local woods to enjoy nature and, perhaps, go fishing.

Nursing was always one of the primary jobs associated with women. The changeover from children being born in homes to the hospitals brought prominence to maternity ward nursing.

Many women found employment working as nursing assistants in nursing homes, passing out medication, food and snacks to residents.

The idea of women serving as nurses and men as doctors was a strictly adhered-to tradition of the time.

Everyday Life

Women at work

The changing culture emerging from the Great Depression was developing a gradual acceptance of women working out of the home.

While women had been generally thought of as nurses or teachers, the emergence of new technology started to open the door for office jobs and certain technical services.

Still many stereotypes persisted concerning "women's jobs" and pay. The opportunities available for women were far fewer than those available to men. There was also some concern about women who worked after they were married and had children.

The growing popularity of air and sea travel offered new opportunities for women who wanted to see the world.

The emergence of telephone party lines opened up switchboard operator jobs for women. Often the operator was a valuable source of information about what was going on around the town.

"One thing you have to say for her—she drives herself as hard as she does old H.J."

Everyday Life

Working on the farm

Farming in 1940 was still marked by the troubles of the Depression and Dust Bowl of the previous decade. The Farm Security Administration, noted for their photographic division, was still helping farmers by subsidizing them and trying to provide education to farmers and their families. However, times were beginning to turn towards the better for those working on farms as the economy improved. Workers began to see hope in owning their own farms again.

Motorized vehicles were helpful tools for farm workers preparing for the harvest.

A much-needed break often included a cup of coffee or a glass of milk for farm workers. Most workers kept long hours on the farm in order to get crops planted and harvested at appropriate times, as well as to maintain a livable wage.

LIBRARY OF CONGRESS, PRINTS AND PHOTOGRAPHS DIVISION, FSA 8C12267

Having working horses was often an essential element of a viable farm. Farmers made sure that they took care of their working animals and livestock.

NEW
DIESEL TracTracTors
by INTERNATIONAL HARVESTER

Now 4 Sizes

A YEAR AGO we announced the powerful TD-18 TracTracTor, a new top for Diesel crawlers. Today International Harvester presents a rugged quartet of streamlined crawlers—TD-18, TD-14, TD-9 and TD-6. FOUR *Diesel TracTracTors* for 1940—big news from the world's leading tractor builder to *all* operators of crawler tractors!

Here's the complete line-up—the big fellow at the right, already a popular favorite in the heavy-crawler field; his little brother at the far left; and the step-ups in between. There's not an ounce of lazy horse-power in any of them! They're ready to tackle their weight in wildcats—each one is ready to lick the crawler-power problem that belongs to his range!

In this complete series of DIESEL TracTracTors, INTERNATIONAL offers you a new standard of performance and economy—perfectly designed balanced power in capacities to meet every demand of the road builder, dirt mover, and general contractor. Standardize on International and enjoy all the advantages only Harvester can provide. Get the full story from any International industrial power dealer or Company branch, or write us.

A great variety of specially designed allied equipment available for all TracTracTor sizes.

INTERNATIONAL HARVESTER COMPANY
(INCORPORATED)
180 North Michigan Avenue   Chicago, Illinois

Companies like International Harvester sought to appeal to the recovering farmers by touting their many-sized and powerful tractors. For those farmers who could afford them, tractors became more and more necessary on the farm.

A man works at a large loom in a textile manufacturing plant.

Here a worker directs a ladle of molten steel into the correct position for emptying into the foundry.

Railroads were key for the steel industry as they provided a convenient and effective method of transporting materials in and out of manufacturing plants. Here iron is unloaded from freight cars.

Textiles and Steel

Manufacturing in America

By 1940, the textile industry was facing a time of decline and diversification. Although textile factories were still largely functioning, leaders of the industry were looking for new avenues to save their plants and keep their workers.

The steel industry, on the other hand, was thriving. As innovations and technology grew, so did the need for steel. Steel manufacturing plants were significant employers in larger cities, like Pittsburgh, which had already established itself as a major producer of steel. Steel manufacturing was also very important as the United States began to ship millions of dollars worth of war material to England and France before German occupation.

The textile industry was still in need of workers who could complete some finishing for their products, like these workers in an upholstery shop.

Everyday Life

Hometown fairs

The annual hometown fair often proved to be the one time each year when people within the community came together to play, visit and find out the latest about each other.

Many communities emphasized the concept of the "street fair." Rides, food stands and the ever-popular "industrial tent," showcasing local businesses with advertising freebies, were located downtown on Main Street. During that time, many of the stores held "sidewalk sales" in an attempt to move merchandise they were eager to sell.

Communities often developed certain theme names for their festivals, many of which represented history-related or heritage traits associated with that community.

Since television was still scarce, locals were often amazed and drawn in masses to certain side shows that brought the extraordinary to the community.

© 1940 SEPS

LIBRARY OF CONGRESS, PRINTS AND PHOTOGRAPHS DIVISION, FSA 8C03327

LIBRARY OF CONGRESS, PRINTS AND PHOTOGRAPHS DIVISION, FSA 8C03330

Competitive activities during fairs were as varied as the communities they represented. School groups and civic organizations regularly faced off with tug of war, barrel tosses and waterball competition.

Street parades were a big part of the fairs. Everyone lined the parade route and waited for business handouts such as candy, fly swatters and yardsticks.

The octopus was one of the favorites on every midway in the 1940s. Youth would make "dares" to see who could be the most hardy on the rides.

Contests, such as those for king and queen and prince and princess, offered youth participation and fund-raising opportunities for local organizations.

"Sure I got the tickets! Where I always put them—in my vest!"

" **WE'RE OFF TO SEE**
This Amazing America!

There was no way to describe the actual experience of seeing sites that, beforehand, had only appeared in magazines and school textbooks.

Travelers wore only the finest dresses and suits when boarding trains and airplanes for cross-country journeys.

Everyday Life

Exploring America

For many, the mental image of such tourist attractions as Washington, D.C., New York City, Gettysburg, Smoky Mountains, Rocky Mountains and California tourist sites were only supplied by verbal descriptions or magazine pictures.

The possibility of automobile trips and passenger train travel opened up a whole new world of personal observation. Those visiting well-known sites would often invite neighbors to their home for pictures and descriptions upon their return.

Hitchhiking also became a popular way of travel, both for tourism and for college students traveling to and from home.

Norman Rockwell

MIAMI

FAMOUS BIRTHDAYS
Martin Sheen, August 3 Actor
Jill St. John, August 19 Actress

Engineering Feats and Disasters

As technology and production developed, so did the erecting of large structures and buildings. An area of particularly large growth was America's roadways. The Pennsylvania Turnpike, the first tunneled United States superhighway, opened on October 1, 1940. The Arroyo Seco Parkway was dedicated in December and became the first Los Angeles freeway. The Queens-Midtown Tunnel in New York opened on November 15.

But not all engineering projects related to transportation were successful. The Tacoma Narrows Bridge collapsed only months after its completion, earning the nickname of "Galloping Gertie" because it oscillated dramatically in high winds.

"Well, shall we chance it?"

The heavy weight of the engine of the Tuckasegee and Southern Railroad train was enough to completely shatter half of the Scott Creek trestle.

Although the Tacoma Narrows Bridge "galloped" since its opening day, nothing could compare to its reaction to the record 42-mile-an-hour winds on November 7, when the suspension bridge snapped and collapsed into the water it spanned. Amazingly, only one car fell into the water. Its driver managed to get out of harm's way before his vehicle dropped. His dog, sadly, became the one casualty resulting from the bridge collapse.

The Pennsylvania Turnpike, initially planned as a Work Projects Administration project to lower unemployment, was such a large undertaking that 15,000 workers were contracted to take part in the construction and 1,100 engineers to take part in the design. The turnpike was a significant enough project that it was featured in the General Motors Futurama exhibit at the 1939–1940 World's Fair.

Everyday Life
School days

Afternoon snacks of milk and fruit or a cookie were often a highlight of elementary school. The celebration of birthdays or special holidays also brought similar special treats to students.

Checking out books from the mobile library gave students an opportunity to choose and read books for their own enjoyment. With the absence of television or high-tech distractions vying for time, many evenings were spent reading.

Special patrol personnel assisted students to the buses when school let out. Excited students could hardly wait to arrive home for involvement in after-school neighborhood sports and games.

REPRINTED WITH PERMISSION FROM CNH AMERICA LLC AND THE WISCONSIN HISTORICAL SOCIETY

© 1940 SEPS

"That new kid must be from California."

Reciting the Pledge of Allegiance and, in some cases, singing the "National Anthem" were part of a daily routine at the beginning of the school day.

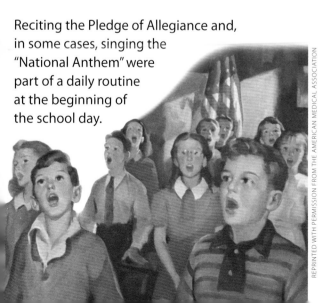

REPRINTED WITH PERMISSION FROM THE AMERICAN MEDICAL ASSOCIATION

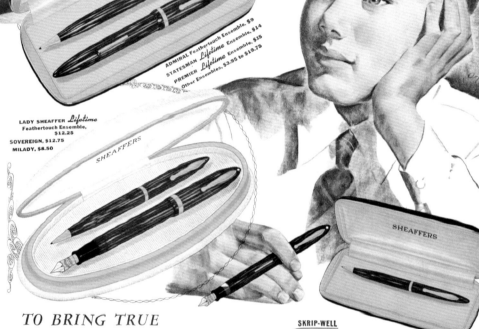

SHEAFFERS

ADMIRAL Featbertouch Ensemble, $9
STATESMAN *Lifetime* Ensemble, $14
PREMIER *Lifetime* Ensemble, $15
Other Ensembles, $3.95 to $19.75

LADY SHEAFFER *Lifetime*
Feathertouch Ensemble,
$12.25
SOVEREIGN, $12.75
MILADY, $8.50

SHEAFFERS

SHEAFFERS

TO BRING TRUE THE DREAMS OF YOUTH

Sentiment . . . faith, love, belief . . . they draw out all our powers, they make us achieve our highest destiny. Neither time nor even death can destroy sentiment . . . But in the fight and the humdrum of daily life, sentiment needs a token, a reminder, to tell us it is there. That is why, when a boy or girl leaves home for school, or a man rounds out 25 years of faithful employment, or a couple passes the 50-year milestone together, it is an American custom to mark the occasion with the gift of a Sheaffer's *Lifetime* Feathertouch, matched with the Fineline Pencil . . . as a daily reminder forever after . . . something to use and cherish every hour . . . the one gift that is equal to the occasion itself.

W. A. SHEAFFER PEN CO., FORT MADISON, IOWA; TORONTO, ONT., CAN.

*Other companies can guarantee their pens for life—some do —but only Sheaffer pens can carry the trade-mark, "*Lifetime*"

SKRIP-WELL

CHEMOPURE
Skrip
WASHABLE, for School and Home
PERMANENT, for Business

Skrip starts faster, dries quicker. Washable washes right out of fabrics. Permanent lasts while the paper lasts—and is sediment-free, non-clogging. Skrip makes ALL pens write better.

Only SKRIP has the SKRIP-WELL—tilt to fill the well—gives your pen exactly the right "drink" no matter whether self-filling or dip type—without soiling pen or fingers! Uses the last drop!

CHEMOPURE SKRIP, successor to ink, 15c. Economy size, 25c.

SHEAFFER'S

All LIFETIME pens are unconditionally guaranteed for the life of the owner except against loss and willful damage—when serviced, if complete pen is returned, subject only to insurance, postage, handling charge—35c.

Copyright, 1940, W. A. Sheaffer Pen Co.

Unless it's SHEAFFER'S *it isn't a* **Lifetime** *- Know the Pen by the White Dot*
REG. U. S. PAT. OFF.

REPRINTED WITH PERMISSION FROM SHEAFFER PEN, A DIVISION OF THE BIC USA

Everyday Life

College life

Attending college was a rather elite experience in the early 1940s. Family expectations still leaned towards a career in agriculture or labor.

In 1940, eight out of 10 boys that graduated from school went to war and more than half of the United States population had completed no more than an eighth grade education. Gender issues were still a problem, as many professors considered young men to have broader vocational opportunities than women.

College was not only a time for learning. Many young men and ladies looked forward to the social opportunities that college life would provide. Whether they were studying together for a test or walking to classes, many co-eds enjoyed spending time with and meeting their fellow students.

© 1940 SEPS

In many colleges, boys outnumbered girls by a large ratio, but it didn't take long to find time to socialize between classes.

REPRINTED WITH PERMISSION FROM SANFORD BRANDS, A NEWELL RUBBERMAID COMPANY

Dress was still quite formal, with ties and accessories being worn in public for guys, and girls still adorning themselves in dresses.

REPRINTED WITH PERMISSION FROM RUSSELL STOVER CANDIES

The Metro Daily News

THE WEATHER
City and State—Fair,
Snow, Colder
Much a few flurries

VOLUME 97 — No. 101

FINAL EDITION

20 PAGES   FIVE CENTS

SEPTEMBER 12, 1940

HERCULES MUNITIONS EXPLODES
The Kenvil, New Jersey plant suffers 55 deaths from explosion.

"No, my ardor hasn't cooled.
I ran out of dough."

The idea of girls having a chance for higher education was slowly edging its way into society; however, most stereotypes still limited girls to teaching and nursing opportunities.

What Made Us Laugh

"He's been ostracized for goose-stepping."

"Come to bed, dear—it's half past December."

"At least you could get a dog with a memory!"

"Your Honor, I have here an elephant."

"Well, the wife thinks you're so smart—
let's see you figure that one out!"

"Of course you're a Republican! All elephants are Republicans!"

"No answer—guess he's not in!"

"I hate to say it, fellows, but it looks like the bottom's
going to drop right out of the panda market!"

Everyday Life
Around the neighborhood

Sprinkles indicating an oncoming shower were often very frustrating after working hard all day to get a wash ready to hang out on the clothesline.

FAMOUS BIRTHDAYS
John Lennon, October 9
musician, The Beatles

"I might be interested.
Here—c'mon in and see me."

The arrival of Father couldn't come at a more opportune time than in the midst of homework. Somehow, there was a hope that Dad could provide a rescue from the boring schoolwork.

The arrival of family and friends was always a welcome sight in the midst of a howling snowstorm. There was something special about cuddling inside a warm home to play games and have hot, satisfying snacks.

"You sure there isn't a <u>motor</u> or somethin', that goes with it?"

Hats were symbolic of style and status. Choosing a hat was a very personal and deliberate decision since the kind of hat a person wore gave others a certain impression of the wearer.

Everyday Life

The well-groomed man

Dressing sharp was a way of life, implying respect for others and pride in personal care. In the 1940s, suits and ties were worn to parties, social outings and for most types of professional meetings.

Accessories were equally important. Tie tacks, cuff links and pins were often used for awards, Christmas and birthday gifts, and identification with certain organizations.

Stylish hats and shoes were usually part of a put-together outfit and were well-advertised items. Shoes in 1940 were often highly embellished and had complicated designs.

better see Roblee
SHOES FOR MEN

Brands and types of shoes were considered to be status symbols. Very few personal-item shelves were not equipped with shoe polish, brush and wiping rags for shoe care.

The Metro Daily News
FINAL EDITION
OCTOBER 29, 1940
THE FIRST PEACETIME MILITARY DRAFT IN U.S. HISTORY BEGINS.

ARROW SHIRTS
SANFORIZED

A trip to the barber shop could often result in much more than just a haircut.

Music

In 1940, the big band orchestra was king in the music world. Glenn Miller topped the charts with hits like "In the Mood," "Tuxedo Junction" and "Careless." Miller, who began playing trombone when he was just a school boy, was already a star by 1940 and continued to dominate the charts over the next few years. Big band leaders like Tommy and Jimmy Dorsey even hired Miller to play with their band. Tommy Dorsey was also a chart-topper in 1940 with his hit "I'll Never Smile Again."

Not all remarkable music events in 1940 related to noted big band leaders. Bing Crosby continued to have success with his popular crooning singing style, maintaining an almost constant place on the music charts. Thelonious Monk, a jazz legend, began playing in 1940, and folk singer and songwriter Woody Guthrie released his first album, *The Dust Bowl Ballads*.

Glenn Miller added to the success of Disney's *Pinocchio* when his hit version of the song "When You Wish Upon a Star" shot to the top of the charts. Although many others recorded the song as well, Miller was the first.

Sitting at home listening to music was a popular activity in 1940. Most radios, like the Crosley radio shown here, at the time were paired with a record player.

Top Hits of 1940

"In the Mood" Glenn Miller

"Frensi" Artie Shaw

"Only Forever" Bing Crosby

"I'll Never Smile Again" Tommy Dorsey

"When You Wish Upon a Star" Glenn Miller

"The Breeze and I" Jimmy Dorsey

"Ferryboat Serenade" The Andrews Sisters

"Careless" Glenn Miller

"Where Was I?" Charlie Barnet

"Ballad for Americans" Paul Robeson

"When the Swallows Come Back to Capistrano" The Ink Spots

"Blueberry Hill" Glenn Miller

1940 brought a collaboration of a music giant, Tommy Dorsey, and a future music giant, Frank Sinatra. That year Sinatra joined the Tommy Dorsey orchestra as a vocalist. Sinatra continued to sing with the Dorsey orchestra until 1942.

Often political figures, like New York's Mayor La Guardia, shown here at left, used the radio to reach the general public over matters such as new regulations, national and local concerns and to post notices.

LIBRARY OF CONGRESS, PRINTS AND PHOTOGRAPHS DIVISION, CPH 3C32498

LIBRARY OF CONGRESS, PRINTS AND PHOTOGRAPHS DIVISION, FSA 8C00054

Radio Shows of 1940

Adventures of Ellery Queen

Edgar Bergen and Charlie McCarthy

Fibber McGee & Molly

Glenn Miller Show

Information, Please!

Kraft Music Hall with Bing Crosby

Lights Out

Mr. Keen, Tracer of Lost Persons

Sherlock Holmes

The Shadow

Tommy Dorsey Orchestra

The radio was a standard fixture in the American home. Children would relax in front of the radio, listening to favorite programs after school. Others would gather to share time together by the radio after dinner. The room that housed the radio became a central area for families to spend the evening.

LIBRARY OF CONGRESS, PRINTS AND PHOTOGRAPHS DIVISION, FSA 8C18174

Radio

Radio was an important part of home entertainment in 1940. People often listened to hear new music releases. Many musicians, like Glenn Miller and Bing Crosby, had their own radio shows. But equally popular were the narrative, comedy, news and variety radio shows.

Some listeners got caught up in the stirring stories of drama serials, anxiously awaiting the next program and becoming emotional along with the characters. Others enjoyed the comedy of Jim and Marian Jordan of *Fibber McGee & Molly*, a long-running show that remained a hit into the 1950s. And still others looked to the radio to keep up on news. President Roosevelt continued to broadcast his "fireside chats" to deliver important information to listeners.

Edgar Bergen and his dummy, Charlie McCarthy, were a popular radio duo and even appeared on several films. Bergen and McCarthy, shown above with the stars from *Fibber McGee & Molly*, attracted many famous guests on their radio show, and appeared as guest stars on other shows.

FDR and his vice-presidential running mate, Henry Wallace, travelled the country to gain voters' support during their campaign.

The Election

FDR on the campaign trail

The 1940 presidential election began with controversy when incumbent President Franklin D. Roosevelt decided to run for a third term. Roosevelt's win over Republican Wendell Willkie led FDR to serve an unprecedented third term in the office of president. Roosevelt was even elected again in 1944, but he passed away only a few months into his fourth term as president. Because of the subsequent passing of the 22nd Amendment, which limits any president to only two terms in office, Roosevelt was the only president in American history that served more than two terms.

In 1940, there were several significant issues that the candidates needed to address in their campaigns. Roosevelt had to fight against voters who believed it had taken him too long to end the Depression. Roosevelt also knew that he needed to appease the mostly isolationist voters by speaking against United States involvement in foreign wars.

"He says a vote is a vote!"

Eleanor Roosevelt, FDR's wife, became well-known herself for her work advocating for civil rights. Eleanor eventually served as a delegate to the UN General Assembly from 1945-1952.

Although choosing FDR to run for a third term was a risky move, the Democratic Party felt that no other candidate had the experience and skills needed to handle the growing threat of Nazi power.

THE SATURDAY EVENING POST

An Illustrated Weekly
Founded A.D. 1728 by Benj. Franklin

5c.
7c. in Canada
(INCLUDING TAX)

September 14, 1940

VOLUME 213, NUMBER 11

19 40

John E. Phillips

© 1940 SEPS

© 1940 SEPS

"I voted for a Republican on three straw votes and four surveys, so this time I'll vote for a Democrat."

Wendell Willkie, a Hoosier born in Elwood, Ind., was familiar with rural America. He had a large following in the Midwest and carried most of the farm vote. Willkie was also known for speaking out against racism and for writing *One World*, a book touting the need for international peacekeeping after the war.

The Election

The challenger

Wendell Willkie, a former Democrat, was considered somewhat of a "dark horse" when he ran for president in 1940 and was a surprise candidate for the Republican Party. Willkie lacked any experience in a political office and was more known for his skills as a businessman and a lawyer than as a politician.

Willkie campaigned against Roosevelt by criticizing Roosevelt's handling of the Depression and by calling for stronger United States support for Allied countries, like Britain. However, Willkie later played to isolationists' fears during the campaign opposing the draft, as well as putting forth the idea that Roosevelt was secretly planning on entering the United States in the war against Germany. Although this tactic did gain him some votes, Willkie still lost the popular vote.

Although Willkie eventually served as a "roving ambassador" for Roosevelt's team, he never actually held any political office. Following his defeat in 1940, Willkie became a supporter of many of Roosevelt's initiatives, including the creation of a military draft , which he initially opposed.

What Made Us Laugh

"Shall I pour?"

"I think we better speak to that new girl in the packing department."

"Run down to the drugstore and call us up, dear. I can't find the telephone!"

"Must be the dentist's bill. It says here: 'Open, please—this is going to hurt a little.'"

"They don't talk—they just get together
and whisper about me!"

"That's just grandma. She's always leaving little notes around."

"This is a tough day for him. The Giants are losing."

"Now I remember where I've seen you before.
It was while we were waiting for this bus."

Favorite stuffed animals and sometimes live puppies were all that was needed to provide a sense of safety to children curling into nighttime dreams.

Everyday Life

Safe and sound

Homemade comforters and blankets from loved ones provided safety and comfort wrapped around those curling into sleep at bedtime. Their warmth was also appreciated in homes where wood fires often burned out during the night.

Stuffed animals such as teddy bears and favorite dolls slept with children to give them a sense of safety during the night.

Favorite bedtime prayers comforted children from fear and assured them that all would be well when they awakened in the morning.

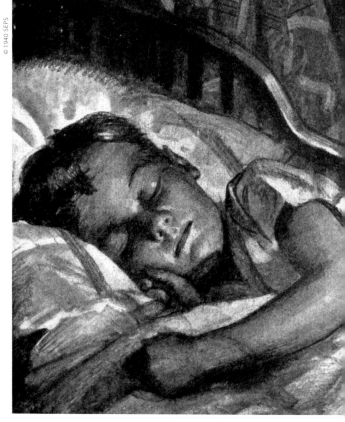

Tired bodies worn out from busy days' activities curled beneath homemade bedding, sometimes with hot water bottles to keep feet warm.

Children who awoke early with a bit of energy often snuck into their parents' rooms to peek at the slumbering adults.

A nap that began over the lull of an engine would sometimes continue while family members visited with loved ones outside the vehicle.

"Guess what?"

Everyday Life

Christmas at home

Homespun Christmases were filled with homemade candies, cookies and fruitcakes. In rural areas, families would often cut their own Christmas tree and decorate it with handmade decorations.

One of the Christmas morning thrills was discovering that Santa had filled stockings that had been hung, traditionally, the night before. In addition to candy, stockings were often filled with small toys and needed items such as pencils, erasers and personal items.

Quite often, extended families gathered on Christmas day, often rotating from home to home on an annual basis for the Christmas present drawing and a carry-in dinner.

"My dad's nuts about pretending he's Santa Claus. So if you see anything, try to be tactful."

FAMOUS BIRTHDAYS
Richard Pryor, December 1
Comedian
Dionne Warwick, December 12
Singer

"Why didn't you yell and tell me you weren't my husband?"

An I[llustrated Weekl]y
[Fo]unded A[. D. 1728 by Benj. F]ranklin

Dec. 21, 1940

Volume 213, Number 25

5c. the Copy

© 1940 SEPS

"All I want to know is what gave you the
idea I wanted the complete works of
Dickens last Christmas?"

"You have to watch this fellow.
Last year he brought me a baby sister."

Everyday Life

Saint Nick

Visiting Santa Claus in a local department store was one of the thrills of the Christmas season for many children. In some cases, stores in close proximity provided Santas, causing some children to wonder how their jolly old friend could get from store to store so quickly. Running into an off-duty Santa was often a confusing surprise for recent visitors.

Some children would spend time writing out a list to hand to Jolly Old Saint Nick. Of course, a treat of a candy cane, orange or maybe even a sack of candy would be given to all of those who visited Santa.

As the lines grew longer, local business owners smiles grew broader as many families would shop for Christmas during the Santa Claus visit.

More *The Saturday Evening Post* Covers

The Saturday Evening Post covers were works of art, many illustrated by famous artists of the time, including Norman Rockwell. Most of the 1940 covers have been incorporated within the previous pages of this book; the few that were not are presented on the following pages for your enjoyment.

THE CRUSH
By
RICHARD SHERMAN

MORE FAMOUS BIRTHDAYS

January 2
Jim Bakker, American televangelist and former husband of Tammy Faye

January 14
Julian Bond, American civil rights activist

January 20
Carol Heiss Jenkins , American figure skater

January 27
James Cromwell, American actor

February 2
David Jason, English actor

February 4
George Romero, American film writer, producer, and director

February 5
H. R. Giger, Swiss artist and Oscar winner

February 9
J. M. Coetzee, South African writer, Nobel Prize laureate

February 12
Richard Lynch, American actor

February 17
Gene Pitney, American singer

February 20
Jimmy Greaves, British footballer

February 24
Peter Deuel, American actor

February 25
Ron Santo, American baseball player

February 28
Mario Andretti, American race car driver
Joe South, American singer and songwriter

March 1
Nuala O'Faolain, Irish journalist and author

March 6
Willie Stargell, African-American baseball player

March 9
Raúl Juliá, Puerto Rican actor

March 15
Phil Lesh, American musician and member of band Grateful Dead

March 17
Mark White, Governor of Texas

March 22
Dr. Haing S. Ngor, Cambodian-American actor and Oscar winner

March 25
Anita Bryant, American entertainer

March 26
James Caan, American actor

March 29
Ray Davis, American musician and member of band Parliament-Funkadelic
Astrud Gilberto, Brazilian singer

April 2
Penelope Keith, British actress

April 12
John Hagee, American televangelist

April 13
Max Mosley, British motorsport boss

April 16
Queen Margrethe II, Queen Regent of Denmark

May 5
Lance Henriksen, American actor and artist

May 7
Jim Connors, American radio personality

May 8
Peter Benchley, American author
Angela Carter, British author and journalist

May 9
James L. Brooks, American film producer and writer

May 15
Don Nelson, American basketball player and coach

May 18
Lenny Lipton, American inventor, songwriter and filmmaker

May 20
Stan Mikita, Slovakian-born Canadian hockey player

May 22
Bernard Shaw, American journalist and television news reporter

June 1
René Auberjonois, American actor

June 2
King Constantine II, former king of Greece

June 16
Neil Goldschmidt, Governor of Oregon

June 20
John Mahoney, British-American actor

June 23
Adam Faith, British singer and actor
Wilma Rudolph, American athlete

July 10
Gene Alley, American baseball player

July 13
Patrick Stewart, British actor
Paul Prudhomme, American celebrity chef and cookbook author

July 17
Tim Brooke-Taylor, British comedian
Verne Lundquist, American sportscaster

July 18
James Brolin, American actor and director

July 22
George Clinton, American musician and member of band Parliament-Funkadelic

August 10
Bobby Hatfield, American singer and member of band Righteous Brothers

August 22
Valerie Harper, American actress

August 28
Tom Baker, American actor

August 29
Bennie Maupin, American jazz musician

September 10
David Mann, American artist

September 11
Brian De Palma, American film director

September 12
Skip Hinnant, American actor

September 14
Larry Brown, American basketball coach

September 18
Frankie Avalon, American singer and actor

September 20
Taro Aso, Prime Minister of Japan

October 13
Pharoah Sanders, American saxophonist

October 14
Cliff Richard, British singer

October 19
Michael Gambon, Irish actor

October 20
Robert Pinsky, Poet Laureate of the United States

October 21
Manfred Mann (Manfred Lubowitz), South African rock musician

October 23
Pelé, Brazilian footballer

October 25
Bobby Knight, American basketball coach

October 27
John Gotti, American gangster

November 12
Glenn Stetson, Canadian singer

November 15
Sam Waterston, American actor
Roberto Cavalli, Italian designer

November 17
Luke Kelly, Irish ballad singer and member of band The Dubliners

November 21
Richard Marcinko, U.S. Navy SEAL and author

November 25
Joe Gibbs, American football coach

November 27
Bruce Lee, Chinese-American martial artist and actor

November 29
Chuck Mangione, famous American flugelhorn player

December 4
Freddy Cannon, American singer

December 21
Frank Zappa, American musician, composer, and satirist

December 26
Edward C. Prescott, American economist, Nobel Prize laureate

Facts and Figures of 1940

President of the U.S.
Franklin D. Roosevelt
Vice President of the U.S.
John Nance Garner

Population of the U. S.
132,122,000
Births
2,559,000

High School Graduates
Males: 579,000
Females: 643,000

Average Salary for full-time employee: $1,200.00
Minimum Wage (per hour): $0.30

NARA, FRANKLIN D.ROOSEVELT LIBRARY

Average cost for:

Bread (lb.)	$0.08
Bacon (lb.)	$0.27
Butter (lb.)	$0.36
Eggs (doz.)	$0.33
Milk (gal.)	$0.26
Potatoes (10 lbs.)	$0.24
Coffee (lb.)	$0.21
Sugar (5 lbs.)	$0.26
Gasoline (gal.)	$0.11
Movie Ticket	$0.24
Postage Stamp	$0.03
Car	$990.00
Single-family home	$2,938.00

REPRINTED WITH PERMISSION FROM GENERAL MOTORS COMPANY

© 1940 SEPS

Notable Inventions and Firsts

January 17: Eleanor Roosevelt publically endorses birth control in a statement that she was not against the "planning of children."

January 31: Ida M. Fuller becomes the first American citizen to receive a Social Security check. Between the years 1937 and 1939, she contributed $24.75. Her check was for $22.54.

March 23: *Truth or Consequences*, a long-running game show hosted by Ralph Edwards, debuts on NBC radio.

April 7: Booker T. Washington becomes the first African-American depicted on a United States postage stamp.

May 15: The first McDonald's restaurant is opened in San Bernardino, Calif. by brothers Dick and Mac McDonald.

June 16: John H. Harris, a Pittsburgh ice rink owner, begins the Ice Capades as a half-time show for hockey games.

July 27: Bugs Bunny makes his first appearance on film in the cartoon short, *A Wild Hare*.

September 11: George Stibitz of Bell Telephone, gives the first demonstration of remote computing when he linked his Complex Number Calculator in New York to a teletypewriter at Dartmouth College and transmitted information back and forth to Hanover from New York.

December 17: During a press conference, Franklin D. Roosevelt first announces his plan, which will become known as Lend-Lease, to send aid to Britain.

© 1940 SEPS

Sports Winners

NFL: Chicago Bears defeat Washington Redskins
World Series: Cincinnati Reds defeat Detroit Tigers
Stanley Cup: New York Rangers defeat Toronto Maple Leafs
The Masters: Jimmy Demaret wins
PGA Championship: Byron Nelson wins

Live It Again 1940

PROJECT EDITOR	Richard Stenhouse
ASSISTANT EDITOR	Erika Mann
ART DIRECTOR	Brad Snow
COPYWRITER	Jim Langham
MANAGING EDITOR	Barb Sprunger
PRODUCTION ARTIST SUPERVISOR	Erin Augsburger
PRODUCTION ARTISTS	Erin Augsburger, Nicole Gage, Edith Teegarden
COPY EDITORS	Amanda Scheerer, Susanna Tobias
PHOTOGRAPHY SUPERVISOR	Tammy Christian
NOSTALGIA EDITOR	Ken Tate
COPY SUPERVISOR	Michelle Beck
EDITORIAL DIRECTOR	Jeanne Stauffer
PUBLISHING SERVICES DIRECTOR	Brenda Gallmeyer

Printed in China
First Printing: 2010
Library of Congress Number: 2009904216
ISBN: 978-1-59635-275-9

Customer Service
LiveItAgain.com
(800) 829-5865

1 2 3 4 5 6 7 8 9